Rookie
Read-About® Health

How Do Your Lungs Work?

By Don L. Curry

Consultants
Jayne Waddell, MA, RN, LPC
School Nurse, Health Educator, Counselor

Nanci R. Vargus, Ed.D.
Assistant Professor of Literacy
University of Indianapolis, Indianapolis, Indiana

Children's Press®
A Division of Scholastic Inc.
New York   Toronto   London   Auckland   Sydney
Mexico City   New Delhi   Hong Kong
Danbury, Connecticut

Designer: Herman Adler Design
Photo Researcher: Caroline Anderson
The photo on the cover shows a simple view of the respiratory system.

Library of Congress Cataloging-in-Publication Data

Curry, Don L.
  How do your lungs work? / Don L. Curry.– 1st American ed.
     p. cm. – (Rookie read-about health)
  Includes index.
  Summary: A simple introduction to the respiratory system.
   ISBN 0-516-25862-1 (lib. bdg.)   0-516-27856-8 (pbk.)
   1. Lungs–Juvenile literature. [1. Lungs. 2. Respiratory system.] I.
  Title. II. Series.
  QP121.C87 2003
  612.2–dc21
                                                    2003004427

CHILDREN'S PRESS, and ROOKIE READ-ABOUT®,
and associated logos are trademarks and or registered trademarks
of Scholastic Library Publishing. SCHOLASTIC and associated logos
are trademarks and or registered trademarks of Scholastic Inc.
12 13 14 R 12 11 10   62

Did you know that you
take about 20 breaths
every minute?

You take even more breaths
when you run or jump.

You breathe in through your nose or mouth.

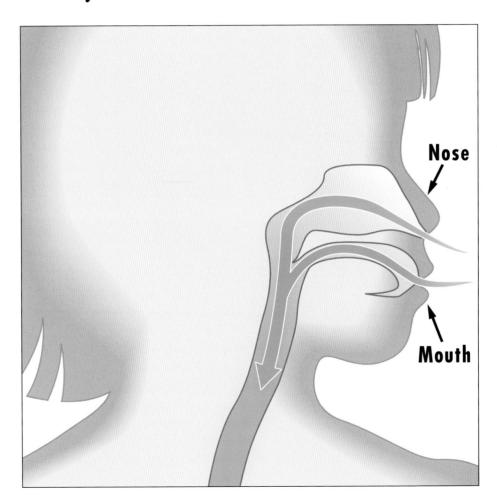

Nose

Mouth

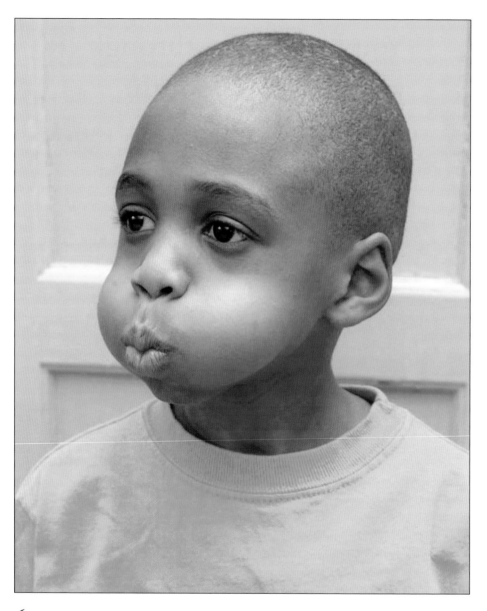

Try to hold your breath.

You might be able to do it for a short time, but not for long.

The air you breathe has oxygen (OK-suh-juhn) in it. Your body needs oxygen to live.

Each time you breathe in, oxygen goes into your lungs.

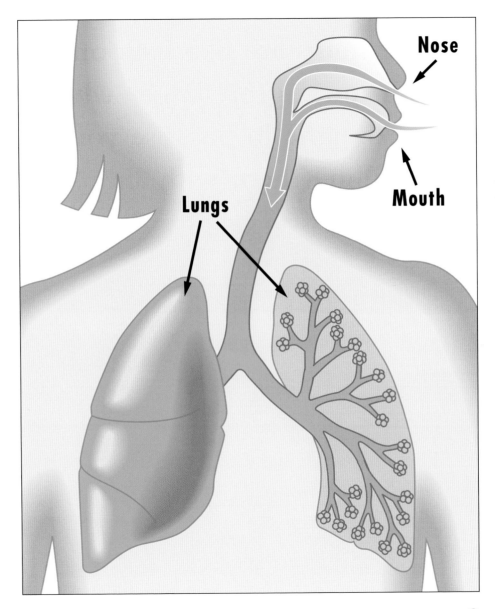

Nose

Mouth

Lungs

Your lungs are like balloons.
Your lungs grow larger when
you breathe in because you
are filling them with air.

Your lungs fill up with air.

Your lungs let the air out.

Your lungs get smaller when you breathe out because you are letting the air out.

You were born with two
lungs. You have one lung
on each side of your heart.

Your lungs take up most
of the room in your chest.

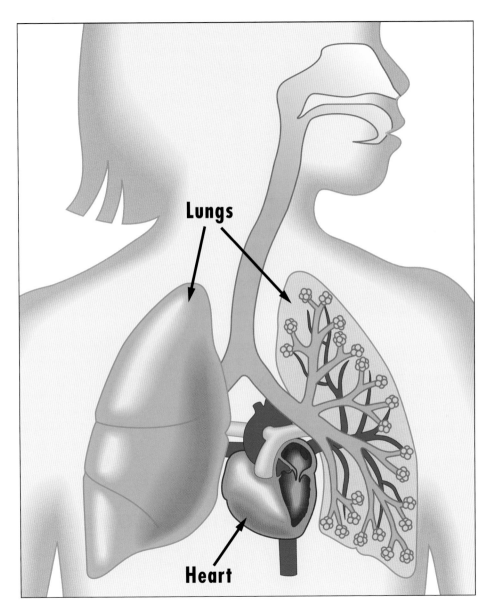

Lungs

Heart

13

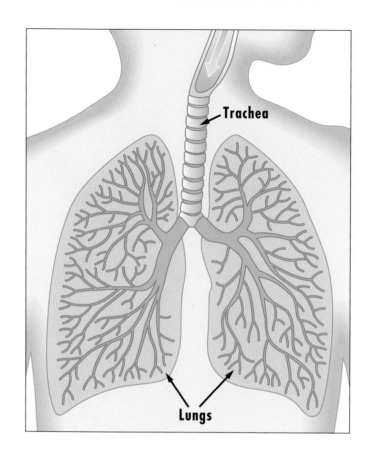

When you breathe in, air goes to your lungs through the trachea (TRAY-kee-uh).

Gently press your finger against the middle of your throat. Do you feel your hard, bumpy trachea?

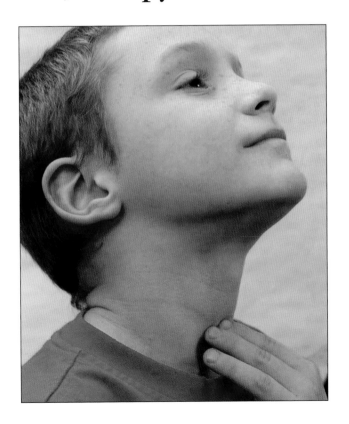

Your trachea splits into two tubes as it goes down into your chest.

These tubes are called bronchial (BRONG-kee-uhl) tubes. Each bronchial tube goes into one lung to fill it with air.

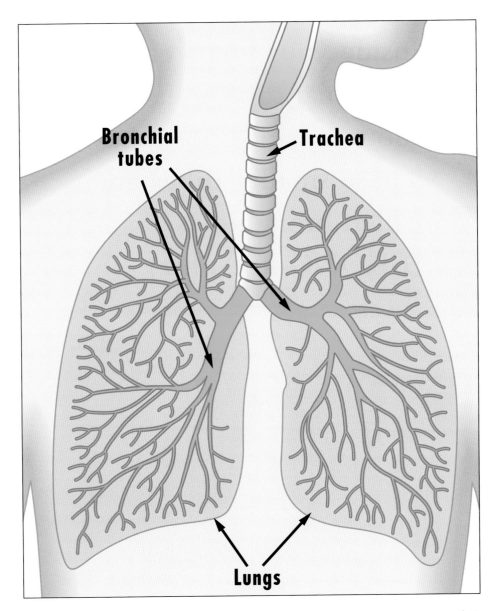

Bronchial tubes

Trachea

Lungs

Inside your lungs each bronchial tube splits into thousands of little tubes. These smaller tubes are called bronchioles (BRONG-kee-ohlz).

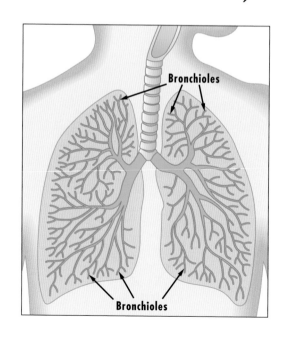

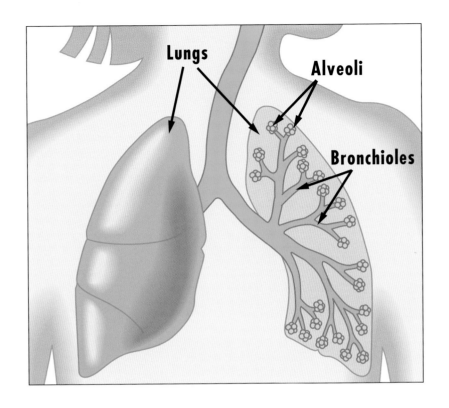

Each bronchiole has a little pouch at the end that holds the air. These pouches are called alveoli (al-VEE-oh-lee).

There are about 700
million (MIL-yuhn)
alveoli in your lungs.

Alveoli look like bunches of grapes.

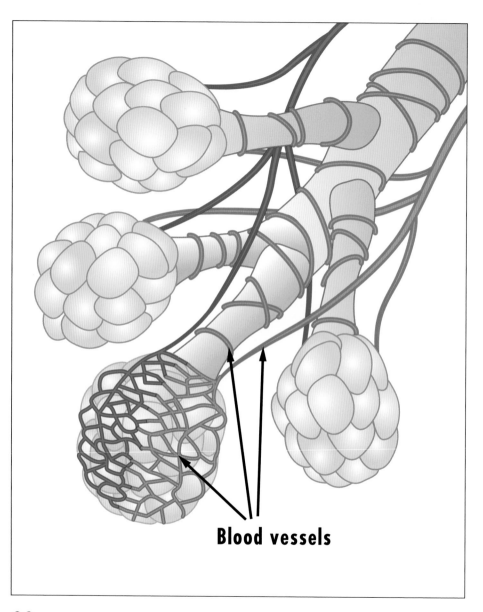

Blood vessels

The alveoli sends oxygen to the rest of your body through your blood.

Blood flows through tiny tubes called blood vessels that cover the alveoli.

The oxygen in the alveoli
mixes with this blood.

The blood carries the
oxygen from the alveoli
to your heart.

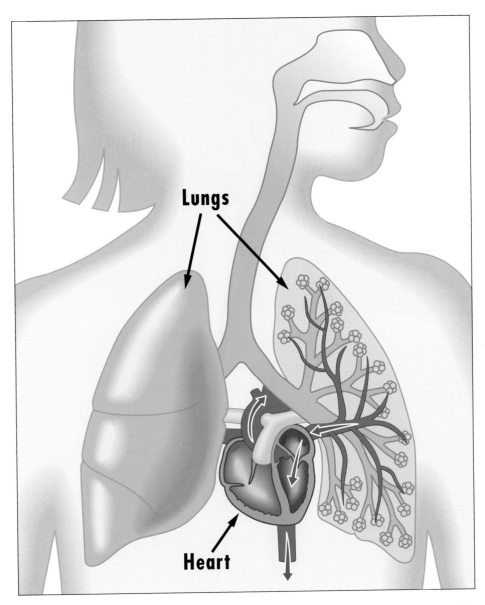

Lungs

Heart

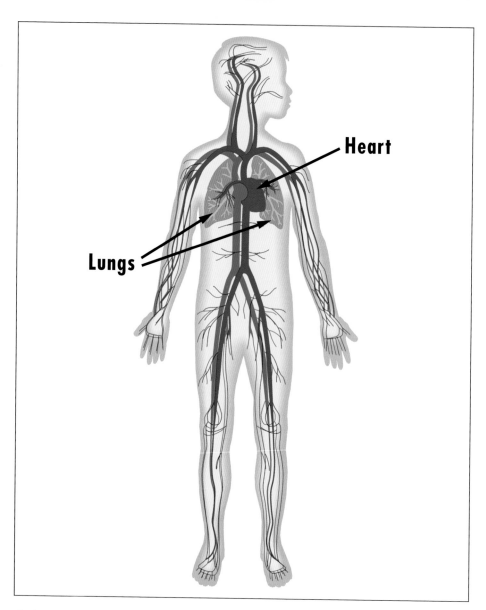

Heart

Lungs

When the blood with oxygen gets to your heart, your heart pumps it out to the rest of your body.

Remember how you could not hold your breath for very long?

That was because your whole body was telling you that it needs the oxygen it gets from your lungs.

Words You Know

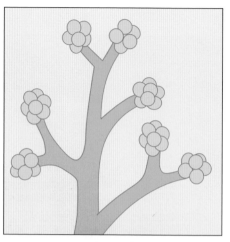

alveoli

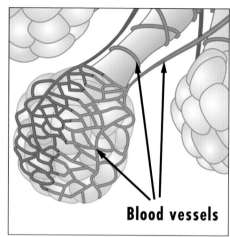

Blood vessels

blood vessels

breath

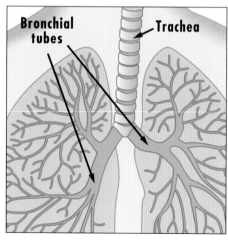

Bronchial tubes **Trachea**

bronchial tubes

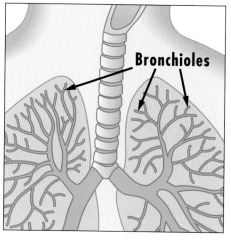

bronchioles

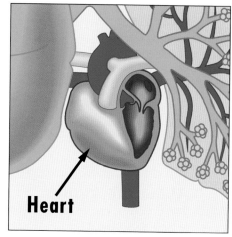

heart

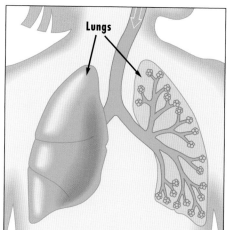

lungs

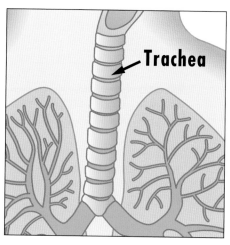

trachea

Index

About the Author

Don L. Curry is a writer, editor, and educational consultant who lives and works in New York City. When he is not writing, Don can generally be found in the park reading, or riding his bike exploring the streets of "the greatest city on earth."

Photo Credits

Photographs © 2003: Ellen B. Senisi: 6, 10, 11, 15, 29; PhotoEdit: 4 (Bonnie Kamin), 3, 30 bottom left (David Young-Wolff); Visuals Unlimited/Eric Anderson: 21.

Illustrations by Bob Italiano